Called to Holiness

CALLED TO

HOLINESS

by
FRANCES
HOGAN

Collins
FLAME

William Collins Sons & Co. Ltd

London • Glasgow • Sydney • Auckland

Toronto • Johannesburg

First published in Great Britain in 1990 by Flame

Flame is an imprint of
Collins Religious Division,
part of the Collins Publishing Group
8 Grafton Street, London W1X 3LA

Printed and bound in Great Britain by
Courier International Ltd, Tiptree, Essex

Called To Holiness

As soon as Christians choose God's way, and turn from all the immorality, materialism and unbelief of the world, they are faced with an altogether new life, and they hear a wholly new call: the call to holiness. This may seem frightening at first, for we humans do not like to be "different" from others. Moreover, this call sets us apart from the majority of those with whom we deal every day as family, friends or neighbours.

A voice cries out in our ears, and resounds in our hearts: "Be holy, for I, the Lord your God, am holy" (Lev. 19.2). Why should we be holy just because God is holy? The answer lies somewhere in the fact that we can only share deeply, and love someone with whom we have some *likeness*. We do not share our innermost depths with those who are not of the same soul as us. If we are to walk with God and share the secrets of His heart then we must in some way become like Him. We must become holy *because* the Lord our God is holy.

Isaiah, the prophet, said that God takes the redeemed on a special path, one that is only offered to those on the journey to salvation and sanctification (theoretically that means all of us): "And through it will run a road for them and a highway which will be called the Sacred Way; the unclean will not be allowed to use it; He (the Lord) will be the one to use this road. . . . it will be used (also) by the redeemed" (Is. 35.8–9). So there is a way to live one's life that is different from that of the world. We have chosen the narrow way taken by the minority. It is this "different" life that we wish to examine.

Yet this road should not be different, for it was

meant for all. The Letter to the Hebrews 12.14 warns us to "seek peace with all people, and the holiness without which no one can ever see the Lord." This New Testament author makes it clear that only holy people will see God in heaven. Exclusion from heaven which is our destiny, is so horrific that it does not really matter what we *call the place*. It's a dreadful thought to consider that if one dies in rejection of God one's *eternal* destiny includes that rejection!

Where will God put all those who die in hatred and bitterness, immorality and lovelessness if only *holy* people get to heaven? In Galatians 5.16–24 St Paul solves the matter, but not to our comfort. He says that those involved in malice and immorality, the occult, idolatry, and behaviour detrimental to others will not inherit the kingdom of God. This is strong language, and demands careful attention, as we shall see.

A HOLY GOD

Even a cursory reading of the Old Testament leaves one with a sense of awe that the all-holy God would get involved with an unholy people and draw them to Himself in covenant relationship so that they became a consecrated nation, a people set apart, a light to the other nations, and a wonder for all time. In order to form a relationship with them He had to reveal Himself for who He really was, and Israel struggled with this revelation for the whole of her turbulent history. We would never know God had He not revealed Himself. Like the unbelievers today we would be left to speculate on the Power behind the Universe, the "Force", "Nature", or fall back on the ancient paganisms of false gods, as many do.

God revealed Himself as holy, utterly other, transcendent, unreachable unless He came to us. Moses discovered this at the Burning Bush (Ex. 3). When God wants to reveal Himself He seeks us out as He did with Moses, as Jesus did with the apostles. Moses witnessed a scientific miracle when he observed a dry thorn bush in the desert on fire (which was nothing unusual, for they could spontaneously combust in the dry burning heat of the desert), but it was not consumed! That was the miracle. Curiosity drove Moses to investigate. Imagine his shock when the voice of God spoke to him from the heart of the fire! God used this situation to get Moses' attention, and to draw him to Himself. The miracle was nothing to God, for He had created the universe just by willing it.

Nevertheless, Moses' introduction to God was frightening: "Moses, Moses!" He said. "Here I am," he answered. "Come no nearer," He said. "Take off your sandals, for the place where you are standing is holy ground. I am the God of your ancestors," He said, "the God of Abraham, the God of Isaac and the God of Jacob." And Moses covered his face, for he was afraid to look at God" (Ex. 3:5–6). Then God revealed his intention to use Moses as the liberator of Israel in the Exodus.

Moses' first introduction to God was His holiness. But what does "holy" mean? In the liturgy of the Mass we say "Holy, holy, holy Lord, God of power and might. Heaven and earth are full of your glory . . .". We proclaim Christ as the all-holy one. We say that saints are holy, that a church is holy; that the priest's vestments are holy; that the scriptures are holy. We keep using this mysterious word which seems to indicate something sacred and pure, not for daily use, not

11

"ordinary". The Hebrew word for holy means to set someone or something apart for God's use. It must be separated from the profane. Hence holy vessels are not touched by everyone, and consecrated people are set apart for the service of God. Consecrated people and things remind us of the "otherness" of God, and of the holiness required to enter His presence.

The holiness of God is inaccessible to humans. He reveals His awesome holiness to special people like Moses, who tell the rest of us, but we would be terrified of the experience that Moses had. He reveals Himself on special occasions known as "theophanies", like the time on Sinai when He revealed Himself to the nation of Israel (Ex. 19.3–20). He also reveals Himself in all His holiness when He comes to chastise His people for being unholy, sinful, unfaithful to His covenant. Such an occasion was the destruction of Jerusalem and the exile to Babylon in the sixth century BC. He reveals Himself through the prophets and saints of both Old and New Testaments. He continuously comes to us in and through holy people, people who live lives worthy of His friendship.

The people of Sinai learned something of the untouchable holiness of God when they were instructed that anyone approaching the mountain that was made holy by His presence, would die. The people had to prepare themselves for three days before they could approach God on the holy mountain. They were instructed to cleanse their hearts, to remain pure, and to wash their clothes (Ex. 19.9–15). On the third day God descended on the mountain in the form of fire, that powerful symbol of life and light and the terrifyingly holy. The mountain was wrapped in smoke, and the people heard thunder and saw lightning as God

communicated with His servant Moses. They shook with fear. The death penalty was waiting for anyone, even priests, who dared approach God without His express invitation (Ex. 19.16–25). Then God decreed the code whereby a people *could* become fit to be His friends. That code was the Ten Commandments (Ex. 20).

They were left in no doubt that God was holy, and that human beings were not fit to enter his presence without His help. That holiness was not just some divine attribute like so many others. It somehow described God in His essence, as Hosea 11.9 says: " . . . for I am God, not man, the Holy One in your midst . . .". This meant that God had an exclusive right to worship and obedience from His creatures, not because He was *in need* of this, but because it put His creatures in right relationship with Him. Obedience to His will, while acknowledging his rights as author and controller of the universe, also enabled Him to guide His people to the fullness of life, and to salvation. Hence obedience to his will is one of the main issues in the call to holiness.

God soon revealed that He wanted a holy people, living holy lives, worshipping a holy God. This would be the great light that He would raise up for all the nations to see, so that other peoples would find their way to the Father also. Hence He prescribed rules of worship, whereby the people could come to Him and be received. He organized a holy priesthood, whose vestments and vessels were consecrated, just as they were. The altar and the Tabernacle had to be consecrated too, so that God could make His dwelling there.

God provided them with a system of worship with some days set apart as *holy days*. On these days they were forbidden to work or carry on normal commerce, for these days belonged to God exclusively. He also gave them special feasts whereby they could continuously celebrate all that He had done for them, and *never forget*. He knew that if they were allowed to forget His goodness to them they would lose their sense of call, and revert to paganism, and this He could not allow.

The very way the Temple was structured reveals the holiness of God. The divine presence was housed in the Holy of Holies in the very centre of the Temple. No one could enter this room except the High Priest on Yom Kippur, the Day of Atonement, for a very short space of time after minute purifications (Lev. 16.1–16). No man would dare enter the divine presence otherwise. This is the awesome side of God.

HOLINESS MADE VISIBLE

The terrible signs of Sinai were not enough if a people were to become attached to God, and live the way he wanted. They had to enter into relationship with Him, and in the ebb and flow of that relationship they would discover very personally who He really was. Since they were a sinful people living in a sinful world how were they to cope with a holy God? Would He not annihilate them when they sinned? There was a hard lesson to learn at the time of the apostasy over the golden calf.

Exodus 32 relates that Moses had gone up the holy mountain again and was in the presence of God for forty days. During this time a dissident group incited rebellion in the whole camp. They prevailed on Aaron, the High Priest, to make a golden calf from their jewellery. They fell to worshipping this work of their own hands (see Psalm 115), and ended their rebellion by feasting in honour of the beast, and reverting to bestial behaviour, for we become like that which we worship. Anyone can tell who our "god" is by our behaviour, which is the bottom line in our service to God. For religion without morality is monstrous.

The holiness of God was outraged. He wanted to punish them, but Moses interceded on their behalf, begging God to show mercy instead. This revealed a new aspect of God's character, for He was willing to deal with a mediator, and He would negotiate. Nevertheless when Moses descended the mountain and saw what was going on he punished them himself, for he was outraged having just come from the august presence of God. He understood the need to express the holiness of God and the abhorrence of idolatry, and its consequent immorality, which was a direct insult to God, quite apart from the fact that it degraded their own persons. Chastisement, therefore, was an unwelcome encounter with the all-holy God.

When ordered by God to move forward on their journey to the Promised Land, Moses learned to his dismay that God refused to accompany them because their sinful and rebellious hearts were an affront to Him, and might provoke Him to chastise them: "Move on towards a country flowing with milk and honey, but I myself will not be going with you or I might annihilate you on the way, for you are an obstinate people" (Ex. 33.3). Moses was dismayed, and the people went into mourning when they realized that God found them disgusting, and unworthy of His presence. This was judgment. The scriptures make it perfectly clear that the punishment for obstinacy and rebellion against God's will is to be denied the Presence of God. When

this happens after death, it is Hell, no matter what physical images we may have of it.

Moses went back to God in prayer, for there was nowhere to go if God did not accompany them. The only thing which distinguished this people from all other people was the fact that the *only true God had chosen to dwell in their midst*. He agonized in prayer for God to reveal a new aspect of Himself to them so that a sinful people could relate to the all-holy God. They did not know enough to deal with the crisis. God, in His wonderful mercy, acceded to Moses' request and revealed new things about Himself that made it possible for sinners of every generation to relate to Him, and to deal with their sinfulness: "Then the Lord passed before him and called out, The Lord, the Lord, God of tenderness and compassion, slow to anger, rich in faithful love and constancy, maintaining his faithful love to thousands, forgiving fault, crime and sin, yet letting nothing go unchecked, and punishing the parents fault in the children and the grandchildren to the third and fourth generation! Moses immediately bowed to the ground in worship . . ." for if God was like *this* they could cope with relating to Him! God would forgive, but would be anxious to educate His people to responsible moral and spiritual living. But once the forgiveness was there, a future existed for this people.

They now realized that God could *feel for their situation* and consequently would deal compassionately with them. His love would be constant and faithful, but also truthful. He would not permit sin to go unchecked, for that would bring about the ruin of individuals, families, and finally the nation itself. For the sake of their survival as individuals and as a nation, He would correct their faults, and show them through the prophets where they were going wrong.

18

Besides, they needed to know the psychological fact that parents automatically pass on their unsolved problems to their children, so it is imperative to deal with reality now, and not leave it to the next generation to clean up after a disaster. Their happy future depended on solving personal and national problems now.

What God revealed here for Moses and the Israelites has application for all of us. Since God never changes, and human nature does not change, our problems today mirror theirs, but in a different setting, and in a more complex society. Moreover, we have the added advantage of hindsight, for we can learn from their mistakes, as we study the scriptures. They have also passed on the solutions they found in keeping God's Word. On top of all this we have Jesus, the Saviour, with us, and the Holy Spirit to enlighten and guide us interiorly on our journey. We have more helps, and are better equipped than they were, so we are without excuse.

RELATING TO A HOLY GOD

What a challenge for an unholy people! God responded by calling prophets and holy men to walk closely with Him, listen to His voice, and learn from Him how to become holy. Otherwise the knowledge of the attributes of God would frighten us, for who could grasp, let alone emulate, His eternity, His majesty, purity, justice, goodness, mercy or His love, to mention but a few? How uncomfortable we feel even at the mention of these great attributes, which contrast so starkly with the conduct of humanity, and show up our unholiness, our lack of likeness to Him.

Yet God made us *for* Himself, and *like* Himself, when He made us in His image (Gen. 1.27) He gave us

19

a rational soul, and the gift of free will, so that we could choose the good and refuse the wicked. He expects all His creatures to have that ability, and to cooperate with Him in growing to physical, emotional and spiritual maturity. He cannot but expect the best of creatures to whom He has given the best that He had, in terms of life, light, grace, redemption, and everything necessary on both the material and spiritual levels. He has given us mental and intellectual gifts, as well as emotional ones, and to crown them and bring them to completion He has given us every spiritual gift through the Holy Spirit. We are without excuse, for life also offers abundant opportunity to grow on all levels.

Holiness is not an optional extra like a hobby that we can pick up if we wish. Neither is it for special people as many say, trying to deceive ourselves. God created us for Himself. We will never achieve true happiness outside of Him who is our true life and destiny. True, we try to achieve happiness through education and all the opportunities that it offers us, but when we reach the height of our achievement what then? Where do we go from there?

Some try to find happiness through travel and adventure, but the weary traveller can reach a point where every other mountain, river, lake, city and people are just mountains, rivers, lakes, cities, people . . . and hassle! Others try music and the arts, but years of dedication leaves them experts who cannot be entertained any longer, for they have become critics. Many try to find contentment through books, achievement, power, pleasure, drink, drugs, the occult, or false religious theories. These latter are more dangerous than the former which at least were healthy outlets. The latter are destructive by their very nature.

No! we were not made for any of these things. We

were made for God, for His glory. We were made to reach for the sky, and know the glory of being sons of God in every sense of that word. Living at the highest level of our being, living the most noble life possible here on earth, we leave behind a testimony to wisdom so that others may find the way. We were made to be like God! Like Him in goodness, purity, holiness, loving concern for others, selflessness, self-sacrifice, a human person fully alive and functioning to the glory of both God and man. Living thus we re-create a little of paradise for those who come in contact with us. Compared to others they are like eagles who soar into the heavens unafraid to look God straight in the face, as it were. Since we have been given the gifts of life and salvation, let us pay any price to become a noble Christian.

A HOLY PEOPLE

Many false notions of holiness abound. Holiness has little or nothing to do with "looking religious", or observing external religious practice (which are good in themselves). It may have little to do with religious experience either, for many who have religious experience become self-absorbed, self-important, maybe even self-indulgent in their prayers and religious practices. It may appear to be holy to have a vision, revelation, or prophecy, but what is the point if we omit obedience to the will of God, which is the bottom line? Or if we are locked up in our devotions when duty calls us to more mundane matters that are essential to life? No, Holiness is separate from an experience of God, just as an experience of golf does not make one a golfer.

Holiness has to do with very ordinary things, and

very ordinary lives! Many people who are truly holy are unconscious of the fact themselves, for it is not a self-conscious thing at all. In fact it is the opposite of self-consciousness. It is God-consciousness, and neighbour-consciousness. It is completely other-centred, quiet, unobtrusive, gentle but very tough. The holy person has said "yes" to life as it presents itself, warts an' all! They are no stranger to the cross, and suffering has become a good friend, although a tough one.

They allow themselves to be moulded by life and the divine providence that governs their daily experiences. They have said "yes" to the circumstances of their lives, and to the people that God gave to them as family, neighbours, and nation. They do not waste precious time lamenting what might have been, or on the giftedness or opportunities of others. They get along using the actual situations given to them, and from this material weave something wonderful to glorify the Lord.

Holy people have the enviable ability, born of long years of prayer, of seeing God everywhere and in everything. This is expressed well in Psalm 139.

> "Lord, you examine me and know me,
> you know when I sit, when I rise,
> you understand my thoughts from afar,
> You watch when I walk or lie down,
> you know every detail of my conduct.
>
> A word is not yet on my tongue
> before you, Lord, know all about it.
> You fence me in, behind and in front,
> you have laid your hand upon me . . ."

This facility to see God everywhere in His creation

brings a great sense of closeness to God, resulting in an increased sense of stability in one's life. It facilitates prayer, since the presence of God is perceived, and He can be contacted anywhere. Since He has the heavens for His throne and the earth for His footstool (Is. 66.1) He needs no special place to be found. He can be found as easily in a church, in His creation, and in His creatures, any time and any place. This brings great relief, consolation and security, and makes the world a friendly home for us: Psalm 139.7–10:

> "Where shall I go to escape your spirit?
> Where shall I flee from your presence?
> If I scale the heavens you are there,
> if I lie flat in Sheol you are there.
>
> If I speed away on the wings of the dawn,
> if I dwell beyond the ocean,
> Even there your hand will be guiding me,
> your right hand holding me fast."

This omnipresence of God is accompanied with a knowledge of his omnipotence. Not only is He everywhere, but He can do anything: "For nothing is impossible with God" (Luke 1.37). Once the realization of his omnipotence dawns on us, then faith opens the door to His intervention in our lives, for we read in Mark 9.24: "Everything is possible to one who has faith". This coupled with the knowledge of God's omniscience, which was referred to in the beginning of Psalm 139, means that we can safely leave the government of the universe to God and His chosen agents, without the temptation to try to become gods to solve everything ourselves. We are able to trust Him who knows and understands all things, and thus remain in peace to do His will.

This is expessed well by Psalm 131:

> Lord, my heart is not haughty
> I do not set my sights too high,
> I have taken no part in great affairs,
> In wonders beyond my scope.
> No, I hold myself in quiet and silence,
> like a little child in its mother's arms . . .

Achieving peace of soul is one of the great fruits of holiness. It is not a refusal to become involved in our world, but the fruit of being properly involved, so that God is allowed *to be* God, and creatures are seen for what they are, creatures, *not* gods. In doing God's will towards our neighbours and our world, we form part of the solution to society, not part of the problem. Besides, we are intercessors, who take their case before the heavenly throne for answers. This loving care for others also increases our peace, since it is fed on love.

Therefore true holiness can be recognized in those who are God-centred, and other-centred, people who are concerned for the welfare of others, to pray, fast and to serve them materially. They are people who project the peace of soul that they experience. The quiet joy that shines from their eyes does not come from a human source, and is independent of circumstances. They are those who accept the cross, still trusting in the goodness of God, and His loving kindness in dealing with us. They have discipline too, for God is a God of order, not chaos, and this calm discipline of God's will rules everywhere in their life. If God wants it, then God gets it at any cost to His servant, who considers it a privilege to be asked.

ENCOUNTERING GOD

The first step is to encounter God in a personal way, as we saw in the case of Moses. Scripture abounds with stories of those who experienced God in such a way that it not only affected their own lives permanently, but also the lives of the nation. Abraham encountered God in the depths of his heart about 2000 BC. He heard the voice of God speak to him to leave his home and country, and begin a new journey of faith. As a wandering nomad Abraham had no one to advise him. He learned to trust God completely from the beginning, and to listen deeply in prayer in order to hear God speak to him. Without any previous knowledge of God, he had to learn to trust God when his faith was tested severely. Abraham became the father of all those who believe on account of his heroic commitment to God under such trying circumstances.

Abraham soon learned that if he was to walk with God that he would have to behave in a way that honoured God, and enabled the Spirit of God to remain with him. He understood that God could not dwell in a house of sin, so the Genesis story reveals Abraham growing in holiness as he learned to walk with God. We discover, for example, his generosity and selflessness with his nephew Lot when the latter took all the good land for himself (Gen. 13). We observe his humility before the priest-king Melchizedech (Gen. 14), yet God tested his trust severely in witholding a son and heir from him right up to old age. How many would have trusted that long? Wouldn't most of us have given up? Abraham trusted God when there was no hope of an answer, and he got the miracle that proved to everyone that God lived. Isaac was that proof.

The original encounter with God was not enough to

sustain a whole lifetime. To live as God required, Abraham needed to commune with God daily in the depths of his heart. He needed further encounters too, deeper ones to serve deeper needs. God came in the way that Abraham could receive him, so we have the lovely account of the three men who appeared at the Oak of Mamre (Gen. 18). They honoured Abraham by telling him of God's intentions with regard to the wicked cities of Sodom and Gomorrah. This set a precedent for future salvation history, as God continued to reveal his secrets to prophets and holy men (Amos 3.7). Abraham was given the opportunity to intercede for the salvation of these wicked cities. They were not to be destroyed before someone prayed for them, so that they would have time to repent, if they so wished.

Abraham persevered in his walk with God, in faith and trust. The big test came when God asked for the sacrifice of Isaac, through whom all the promises were to be fulfilled (Gen. 22). Why was this? God knows that we are unaware of the condition of our hearts until we are tested. The test shows up what is inside, unknown to all others, sometimes even to ourselves also. The test for Abraham, as for all the saints who followed him, was this: would you choose God to the loss of everything? Would you give to God what is most dear to you? The test uncovers what that "most dear" person or thing or experience is. For Abraham it was his son, whom he loved dearly as the only child of his marriage to Sarah, the miracle-child, the child of promise. Most dear also because he was the child of their old age.

To offer Isaac to God was the supreme act of worship which proved that Abraham put God before all creatures, no matter how beloved and close. It proclaimed

God's supreme rights over all His creatures, and gave glory to God. The Letter to the Hebrews (11.17–19) says that in offering Isaac to God, Abraham believed that God would give him back from the dead in order to fulfil His promises, since God cannot lie. What He says He will perform. This was an extraordinary act of faith and hope in one who lived so far back in time. Has he been surpassed very often? I think not! He set a very high standard for all who would follow.

REFUSING THE CALL

Abraham, Moses, Isaiah and many other holy men named in the scriptures said yes to the call of God. Is it possible to receive a call and refuse it? Is it possible to encounter God in a real way, and yet turn away? Unfortunately yes! Let us learn from a few such cases. The synoptic gospels relate the story of the rich aristocrat who came to Jesus and offered his services to the kingdom of God. He was a good living person, who kept the commandments. He was not just rich: he was religious also, and thought to put his money into the service of the kingdom. Very worthy sentiments, but watch Jesus' reaction. It's not money he wants, but people!

In his response Jesus tried to reach the heart of the man who addressed him thus: "Good Master, what shall I do to inherit eternal life?" This was the wrong question, for it relied on deeds rather than a relationship with the Saviour that would bring about his own sanctification and the service of others. Because he was rich he could finance a project which might make him feel good, but might not *make* him good, because the good deed might build up his pride and self-satisfaction in his achievement, and prevent his opening his heart to salvation. This was a tragedy that Jesus would prevent if he could.

Jesus called upon the man to reflect on his request: "Why do you call me good? No one is good but God alone". Obviously the man considered himself good, because he kept the commandments, and did not yield to immorality, unbelief and worldliness. To the eyes of the world he certainly *was* good! But this very goodness of his was preventing him from seeing his need of a saviour. It was blinding him to his own self-sufficient pride that blocked out the grace of God. He had not felt need of God, or of change, even of growth. He thought he was fine! Jesus questioned him on those commandments that deal with duty to our neighbour, but the man claimed he was faultless. He had never done any wrong. He had kept away from evil, but *had he done any good?*

Very gently and delicately Jesus said: "There is still one thing you lack". If he was only lacking in one thing he must be next door to perfect? But no! He lacked the *only thing he should have done*, which was to love his neighbour as himself. His religion was legalism, not love. But God is love, and the kingdom of God is a kingdom of love. Love is the one law of that kingdom, and Matthew 25 makes it perfectly clear that we will be judged on love in the ultimate encounter with God. The man lacked what was essential to be holy, and a friend of God. He needed urgent repentance if grace were to transform him.

Jesus said: "Sell everything you own and distribute the money to the poor, and you will have treasure in heaven; then come, and follow me." Jesus asked this man to give away what was dear to him, to make a

choice between God and material things. This would show God that he loved him, as he claimed to do in keeping the commandments. But most people want God *and* other things. They don't want God exclusively, for Himself alone. Some, like this man, want God but not their neighbour, for they may be prejudiced against them. They want God but they *also* want comfort, pleasure, worldliness and all that money can buy. They say that after all we should not be fanatics!

In behaving thus they are very unlike Abraham and Moses, who chose God to the loss of everything, when asked. Jesus told this young man that he would have treasure in heaven only if he used his riches to benefit others. His treasure was on earth now, but he was very attached to it. In his case Jesus would not even consider him a candidate for discipleship unless he rid himself of all that kept him back from God, from life, and from encountering his neighbour in a life-giving relationship of loving service. He was a poor rich man. All he had was money.

This young man received a *real* call from a *genuine* encounter with God, in Jesus: but he rejected it, and walked away sad "for he was very rich". All he had was his money and what it could purchase, but he forfeited eternal life for its sake! There are serious consequences to rejecting grace, and this too we must look at. Luke 16.9 gives very important information for solving this man's problem: "And so I tell you this: use money, tainted as it is, to win you friends, and thus make sure that when it fails you, they will welcome you into eternal dwellings". Using the wealth as Jesus suggested would have been an important step on the road to holiness for this young man. It would have freed his heart to serve God, and given him the privilege of giving joy to so many. Nevertheless, the man was free, and he freely chose to reject Jesus' offer, and the new life that it entailed. That is our privilege, but we must live out the consequences of our decision.

THE CASE OF JUDAS

Judas is one of the most tragic cases in the Bible of the rejection of a call from God. Unlike Abraham and Moses, Judas met God Incarnate. He met God personally in Jesus of Nazareth. Jesus called him to become, not just an ordinary disciple, but one of his chosen few, an apostle. This was an absolutely unique privilege for a follower of Jesus. Judas was a young man when he joined Jesus' group of disciples. He said yes initially, and so one would expect that all would be well from then on. But no! Judas reveals that it is possible to be *in something but not of it*. He followed Jesus, and as far as anyone outside could see he was the same as the others, but Jesus said: "By their fruits you shall know them" (Matt. 7.15–20).

The gospel gives no details of Judas' initial call, or how he met Jesus. It merely relates that he was numbered among the Twelve when Jesus officially appointed them to speak and work in His name. It was to this group that he gave the power to heal and to cast out devils. He appointed them "to be his companions" (Mark 3.13–19). Judas was given the same gifts, graces and opportunities as Peter, who eventually became the head of the mission team to all the world. Also John, who became the disciple who knew Jesus best, and who was best loved by him.

The destinies of these three men depended on their relationship to Jesus, and their correspondence with grace. It is well known that the impulsive and fiery Peter needed a lot of transforming grace in order to become useful to Jesus and the kingdom of God. So there is no excuse for Judas, as he had the same Saviour, the same divine friend, the same call, the same opportunities, the same salvation, the same teaching, etc. What was the difference?

The essential difference is something known only to God at its root stage, but becomes obvious to all when it matures into action. It appears that Judas did not let the teaching of Jesus *change his way of thinking*. He accepted that Jesus was the Jewish Messiah, but like most of his generation he understood this on a purely human and natural level. This meant that his concept of that Messiahship was political, and would involve a power struggle with Rome eventually. This concept of Messiah saw him merely as a human being like ourselves, with no special dimension of divinity. Therefore Judas *never penetrated the mystery of the person of Jesus*. And this because of his own mind-set that would not shift, no matter how much evidence was given.

Further, Judas would interpret the teaching of Jesus on the level of his own mind-set, instead of hearing what Jesus actually said. This is an all too frequent occurrence with human beings. Because of preconceived ideas we do not perceive the reality around us, and like Judas, we can miss a major visitation of God in our lives. It is frightening to consider how close this man was to God in the physical sense, and how little he benefited from it. Unlike him, Peter and John allowed Jesus to train them in holiness, and selfless service to their fellow-man, and they became famous world leaders. Judas, on the other hand, became a world tragedy, too terrible to think about.

Yes, we must face the fact that we can reject grace, and bring about our own ruin in so doing. We are the authors of our own destiny, and may not blame anyone else for our failure to live and use all the opportunities that life offers us to grow in every area of our lives. Holiness is offered to all. Grace and salvation are offered to all. Opportunities to grow are given to all, since God is no respecter of persons. What we do with this call, this grace, this salvation is up to us, but God who is just as well as merciful, holds us responsible for our free choice, and its consequences, and deals with us accordingly.

IS JUDAS A "ONCE-OFF"?

Unfortunately Judas was not to be the last to deny Christ. No, just the first in a long line over the centuries of Church history. St John (1 John 2.18–19) says that even in his day several Antichrists had come: "Those rivals of Christ came out of our own number, but they had never really belonged . . . ". John warns Christians that it is possible to be in the Church and yet live like a traitor, because one refuses to do what the Lord asks. He says in 1 John 2.15–16 that we "must not love this passing world or anything that is in the world." Why? Because "the love of the Father cannot be in any man who loves the world, because nothing that the world has to offer—the sensual body, the lustful eye, pride in possessions—could ever come from the Father but only from the world . . . "

Judas' sin was to continue to live a worldly life regardless of the grace offered him by Christ. He refused to change his way of thinking to that of Christ, and therefore he did not live by Christian principles. In

the text above, John said that the love of God cannot reside in such a person, and this is serious, for our salvation is at stake.

Many Christians today are like Judas in that they think they have the right to live a worldly, sensual life, in which their own ego is at the centre. They must have everything they desire, even to wanting to change the rules to make this happen. "I want" rules their lives and decides their value systems. Nevertheless they expect that attending church services and saying a few prayers legitimizes it all. No! This is wrong thinking, for Jesus said in John 14.15: "If you love me you will keep my commandments", not change them to suit your own personal wants. And in 14.23 he continues: "If anyone loves me he will keep my word", not change it just because someone wants to change their partner! There are very definite demands made upon us. Here, as in life generally, we are not permitted to "have our cake and eat it".

Luke's gospel (12.47–48) makes it clear that judgment awaits that servant of the Lord who does not carry out the Master's wishes. God holds us responsible for our decisions and our behaviour. With regard to this Jesus said: "The servant (the Christian) who knows what his master (God) wants (obedience to the commandments, and to God's will in general), but has not even started to carry out those wishes, will receive very many strokes of the lash (judgment). The one who did not know, but deserves to be beaten for what he has done, will receive fewer strokes. When a man has a great deal given him, a great deal will be demanded of him . . ." Christians in general have had a great deal given because we have salvation in Christ; we have his word, his presence in the Eucharist, the Church, etc.

And this apart from all the personal gifts we have been given. Truly a great deal, in terms of generous response to God's kindness, is to be expected.

Will Judas be the only one left out of the final glory? St Matthew says very clearly in 24.50 that "as for the dishonest servant (Christian) who says to himself, 'My master is taking his time' (the Second Coming is a long way away), and sets about beating his fellow servants and eating and drinking with drunkards (loses faith and becomes worldly), his master (Jesus) will come on a day he does not expect and at an hour he does not know. The master will cut him off and send him to the same fate as the hypocrites (those living a double life), where there will be weeping and grinding of teeth." This weeping and grinding of teeth is a very good description of the absolute frustration of people who find themselves permanently outside the presence of God eternally.

The parable of the talents in Matthew 25.14–30 reiterates this teaching, and it is followed by the scene of the final judgment in which Christians do, in fact, find themselves sent off to Hell for not caring for their neighbours. This refusal to serve the neighbour is a definite refusal to obey Jesus' special command in John 13.34: "I give you a new commandment: love one another; just as I loved you, you also must love one another. By this love you have for one another, everyone will know that you are my disciples." Many people today think of this command to love as a soft "lovey-dovey" thing. They say that all you need is love, and they are right, if they understand the awesome responsibility that it entails.

Our generation wants love without responsibility. It is a sensual, self-indulgent generation that knows little or nothing about the glorious side of love, which is the faithful, loving service of the neighbour at any cost to oneself. It does not understand pure love, which is utter self-giving, even to the laying down of the life. Consequently it does not understand God, when it is told that God is love. It measures God by the self-indulgent society, and therefore says that God is *so good* that there can be no Hell. But this is ridiculous, for love is righteous and just, as well as merciful and kind. Above all love is holy, awesome, pure and purifying. It is the divine fire that Jesus wanted to cast upon the earth to purify it and make it worthy of God's most holy presence.

When we measure God by our standards we not only diminish God, but we insult Him also. There will be judgment for all the Judases because God is holy and just, and He remembers the millions of other human beings who were not given our privileges and graces, and who if they were given them would have used them with profit. See Luke 13.22–30, where Jesus warned the religious leaders of his own day that they would find themselves left outside the kingdom of God, while tax collectors, public sinners and Gentiles would take their places. This is real, and we must take heed.

REVOLUTION IN OUR THINKING

As we face into the third millenium St Paul's advice to the Romans (13.11–14) of his day is very urgent: "Besides, you know 'the time' (the end-time) has come: the moment is here for you to stop sleeping (in worldliness and sin) and wake up (spiritually), because by now our salvation is nearer than when we first began to believe. The night (of human history) is nearly over, daylight (eternity) is on the way; so let us throw off everything that belongs to the darkness (evil), and equip ourselves for the light. Let us live decently, as in the light of day; with no orgies or drunkenness, no promiscuity or licentiousness, and no wrangling or jealousy. Let your armour be the Lord Jesus Christ, and stop worrying about how your disordered natural inclinations may be fulfilled."

The early Christian teachers were in no doubt that if the Christians took their example from the way the world was living they would end up in the same condition as the world, namely, full of doubt, unbelief and its consequent immorality, as we observe all around us today. The Christian way is very different. It is based on very different principles. Instead of self-indulgence, the disciples of Christ use self-restraint in their behaviour, so that their response to their neighbour is governed by God's law and by Jesus' special demand of charity, or God's love, not by passing sentiment. This is an other-centred life as opposed to a self-centred, self-indulgent one. They are diametrically opposed, as are their fruits.

St Paul "compared" them graphically in Galatians 5.19–22 where he describes the life of the flesh versus the life in the Spirit. Once the comparison is given the decisions facing us are too clear to need comment. Paul compares them to two bunches of grapes. One bunch is good and healthy, the other is bad. What caused the decay? Paul says that the root of a wicked life of sin is self-indulgence. Here is the fruit of such a life: "When self-indulgence is at work the results are obvious: sexual vice, impurity, and sensuality [which have reached epidemic proportions in western society], the worship of false gods and sorcery [which are very rampant today]; antagonisms and rivalry, jealousy, bad

40

temper and quarrels, disagreements, factions and malice, drunkenness [behaviour considered quite normal today], orgies and such things. And about these, I tell you now as I have told you in the past, that people who behave in these ways will not inherit the kingdom of God." The frightening aspect of this scenario is that it describes the world of today, as it goes its merry way in ignorance of the presence of the all-holy God, who sees and knows everything that occurs.

The life of grace is completely the opposite of this: "On the other hand the fruit of the Spirit (the action of grace in our lives) is love, joy, peace, patience, kindness, goodness, trustfulness, gentleness and self-control; no law can touch such as these. All who belong to Christ Jesus have crucified self with all its passions and desires." It is not difficult to see that living with a person who behaves according to the Spirit is a wonderful experience, a touch of paradise, whereas living with the types illustrated in the last group would be hell on earth. Hence to shift from one to the other is, quite literally, a revolution in our thinking, a miracle of grace. Yet that is what salvation is all about!

THE CATERPILLAR

Let us illustrate it by looking at the making of a butterfly. The caterpillar must die in order to become a butterfly; the lesser life must give way before the higher life just as the old man in us must give way before the new man in Christ. The lower nature must yield to the higher nature if we are to be more than just animals. Nature must give way to grace if we are to respond to the call to holiness. This is not so much a process of dying as a process of transformation.

The caterpillar crawls on the ground, with its vision too narrow and limited for a higher life. Its existence is self-centred. It spends its time eating and growing, with no reference to other life forms around it. This process is so engrossing that it is unaware that it leaves a trail of destruction in its wake. One can trace it through the partial use of all the greenery in its path. This can be seen as a symbol of the irresponsible use of the resources of life. Besides, its life is both sluggish and slow. It is a consumer, not a producer.

Nevertheless, if it agrees to die to itself, it can be transformed into a very useful butterfly, and it will also be freed from all its constraints. It must weave a cocoon around itself, and cease all its former activities to concentrate its energy on the transformation of its whole being. Patience, time, and the mysteries inherent in nature will do the rest. At the due time it emerges into a whole new life as a glorious butterfly, able to fly over all the places where it crawled before. Its ability to fly gives it a greater vision of life and its possibilities. It is now gloriously free. No longer does it leave a trail of destruction in its wake. On the contrary, it gives an essential service to flowers who depend on it for their life processes.

The caterpillar had to change in order to get its wings, and so do we, if life is not to fall on top of us a heavy weight that we cannot sustain. We must be transformed even for the sake of all other creatures inhabiting the planet, if we are not to continue to leave a trail of destruction behind in the deforestation of whole regions of the earth, in the destruction of species of animals every year, and of the environment itself. The other creatures need us, but as people who can fly spiritually, thus gloriously manifesting God's presence

in love and holiness, and restoring paradise to all. Romans 8.19–21 says this clearly: "the whole creation is waiting with eagerness for the children of God to be revealed . . . (so that it) might be freed from its slavery to corruption and brought into the same glorious freedom as the children of God".

This transformation must be seen as vital both for individuals and nations, and as an essential service to the human race. Nature is filled with parables which proclaim the need for this death/life process. Jesus used one in John 12.24–26 referring to his own death/ resurrection mystery which was to make transformation into holiness possible for everyone. "In all truth I tell you, unless a wheat grain falls to the ground and dies, it remains only a single grain; but if it dies it yields a rich harvest. Anyone who loves his life loses it. Anyone who hates his life in this world will keep it for eternal life."

Here we are asked to consider the short- and long-term effects of our life decisions. If we live for the world and the flesh exclusively, then we do so at the cost of our salvation. But if, for the sake of the greater good, we are prepared to sacrifice temporary and ephemeral things in order to take care of the kingdom of God, we gain eternal life. In other words the loss is temporary but the gain is eternal. But if we live for the flesh only then the loss is eternal and the gain is even questionable in the short term.

WHAT ARE THE MEANS TO GROW IN HOLINESS?

If a person decides now to respond to the call of God, where do they begin? Where do they go? First of all, let us assert clearly that while growth in holiness requires our full cooperation, holiness is God's gift and flows from him. The first step is to encounter God and then to remain in His presence. It is God's presence in our lives that transforms us, gradually changing us into the image of Christ, His perfect Son (2 Cor. 3.17–18). It is not the things that we do that makes us holy. It is what God does in and through us as we endeavour to do His will in our lives on a daily basis, in ever greater detail, and with greater love and humility.

Something is called "a means to holiness" if it puts us in contact with God, and somehow feeds the growing relationship between God and His people. It opens us up to the operations of the Holy Spirit in our lives, and thus keeps us close to the source of holiness, Jesus Himself. The means to holiness are the following: the Church, the Sacraments, the Eucharist, personal prayer, the holy scriptures, daily divine providence, keeping the commandments, doing the will of God, service to one's neighbour and carrying one's cross in union with the Lord. And this is not an exhaustive list.

THE CHURCH

This is the living community of believers who support one another in seeking and following the Lord, and in the service of humanity. They are that special group of people who have agreed to cooperate with the Lord in spreading and servicing the kingdom of God on earth. They also preserve the teachings of the Lord intact, and endeavour to carry them out faithfully. Jesus has given to his Church clear teaching authority to enlighten and guide us towards holiness and truth. He did not leave his disciples to find their own way through the desert of life, but made sure that they would have brothers and sisters to give fellowship and support to them. The candidate for holiness finds in this body of believers wise and holy people who can guide their steps in the ways of the Lord, both by teaching and example. Here, too, the erring disciple will find loving correction that ensures that they do not stray from the path of salvation.

It is extremely dangerous for someone wanting to grow in holiness to remain isolated from the Christian community, for there are dangers too great for the individual to handle, and temptations too difficult to resist. To "go it alone" spiritually is madness, for even Jesus was assailed by the devil when he dared to spend forty days in the wilderness alone. The devil is absolutely determined that none of us will see heaven. He lost his place there through pride, and he works unceasingly to prevent us from reaching our destiny too. It is not so much that he hates us individually, but that he hates Christ, and wants to rob him of the fruits of his sacrifice. Jesus paid for our heaven with the price of his life, and the devil wants to prevent this joy being given to him. We must endeavour to cooperate with Christ to not only go to heaven ourselves, but work with him to bring as many others with us as possible. This we do most effectively in the Church surrounded by other believers, and co-workers in the kingdom of God.

THE SACRAMENTS

The second means to grow in holiness is to use the sacraments wisely and well. These are seven signs of grace given by Jesus to his Church whereby the fruits of his death and resurrection can be applied to our lives in time of need. They correspond to the needs of life

itself. They begin with Baptism which gives us new life in Christ for the first time. The person is reborn in Christ, a new person with the life of grace given to them gratuitously by God. The gift of the Holy Spirit is given for the first time here also, and it is from this wonderful initiation that we begin the journey to God and salvation. We are now born of God.

As a consequence of Baptism the new Christian needs to grow and mature. Spiritual food is provided from two sources, the Eucharist, and the holy scriptures. The Eucharist is the source of all spiritual life, for through it we feed on the Lord Himself. Jesus loved us infinitely, with God's own love. Therefore he provided us with celestial food, for a spiritual life requires heavenly food. To this end he gave us his own flesh and blood for our nourishment. Moreover, in the sacrament of the Eucharist we encounter God personally, and intimately. There can be no greater privilege for a mortal than this. When the woman with the haemorrhage in the gospel touched the hem of Jesus' cloak and was instantly cured, that was a very outward and superficial encounter when compared to the Eucharist.

When we receive Jesus in the Eucharist we are encountering him as the Risen Lord of Life, victorious over all the forces of evil. This, therefore, is the time to intercede for the world and its needs, to become a missionary in our prayer. This encounter with Jesus in the Eucharist is so deep that it is not a felt experience. Some things are of a higher order than what the flesh can register. One must seek illumination from God with regard to its reality. Knowing the doctrinal facts is not enough. One needs enlightenment here.

The grace received in the Eucharistic encounter is such that it cures illnesses for those who open up to allow the Lord to operate on this level, for God is the same yesterday, today and forever. The person we meet in the Eucharist is the same Jesus who healed the sick and raised the dead in Palestine 2,000 years ago. The Eucharist also cures faults and purifies us of sinfulness, and is altogether the greatest means of growing in holiness. At the moment of receiving the Eucharist each one of us becomes the Beloved Disciple leaning on the heart of the Lord, and there we have his exclusive attention and love. In that moment of intimacy we whisper the name of the friend, family, country or people that we wish him to bless, and he will do it just because we asked!

THE WORD OF GOD

The other great food is The Word of God. The Lord loves His people so much that He left us His own word to be a guide on the path of holiness and life. There we find all the instruction needed to find our way, and to come back after we have strayed. There we find examples to imitate, and others to take warning from. We find too, that the Lord has left us teaching on prayer, and a whole hymn book that expresses every human emotion to God. He has put words into our mouths lest we have the excuse that we cannot pray. That wonderful prayer book, the Psalms, also shows us that our personal struggles are not unique, for every traveller on the road has had them, and many were worse than what we have to go through. Other people's crosses are heavier than ours, so we become grateful to God for being so lenient to us, a thing we might not have understood had we not read His holy word.

We should read God's Word with the same interest

and eagerness that worldly people read the daily newspapers! There they read all the bad news of the day, the scandals in high places, and the reviews of journalists who may not have any insight into life or reality. God's Word, on the other hand, is full of insight into life and reality, and the commentators are all inspired by the Holy Spirit so that we can trust their point of view. It has that something extra that puts it on a different plane to an ordinary piece of writing.

For the child of God on the way of holiness, reading scripture is a daily event, where they read this wonderful letter from the divine Father of humankind who explains how humans "work", the whole message of salvation, and why disasters happen and how to prevent them, as well as commenting on the political affairs of the days of the writers. On reading this one realizes that there is nothing new on the earth, but that history repeats itself. Learning from it, we can become wise with real insights that help others find meaning in their lives, and direction to find the way of Truth.

Besides, the Christian finds that scripture reveals the will of God clearly and unambiguously, so that they know what God asks of them. They will grow in peace as they learn to put the will of God into effect in their daily lives. An example of how clearly the scriptures manifest the will of God is Luke 6.20–49, where we are told to love our enemies, to give generously, to lend without any hope of return, to be compassionate, not to judge, etc. The problem here is obedience, not understanding. One understands what is being asked only too well! Since human nature does not like what is asked, prayer becomes necessary, in order to receive strength and courage to carry out what has been clearly demanded. When people claim that they do not know

the will of God you may be certain that they are not reading the holy scriptures!

Very soon on the journey one needs to discipline one's day to make room for daily scripture reading. It needs to be disciplined reading too! There is little fruit derived from reading in a haphazard way that leaves one with no concept of the overall meaning of a book. If you are a beginner then use the principle of going from the known to the unknown. This means that you should begin with a thorough reading and study of the gospels, then the Psalms as both of these areas are widely used in church and familiar to everyone. After that use you own discretion, but a scripture class will be helpful to gain deeper understanding, and will aid perseverance. The majority find they need the scriptures explained to them.

FORGIVENESS

The growing person makes mistakes and falls along the way, so it is necessary to get the Lord's medicine of forgiveness and healing love. The Sacrament of Reconciliation which is so little understood in our permissive society where "anything goes" is, in fact, a great means of holiness, for it is there that we expose our woundedness to the Lord for healing and strength. There, too, we continuously hear his loving words of forgiveness no matter how often we fall. Further, we see the delicacy of his love, where he wants us to be sure, through the words of a fellow traveller, that he is really with us in all our troubles. Finally, it is there that he gives a compassionate ear to all our woes, and offers us his healing grace. It is unwise to omit this spiritual bath, whereby the Lord cleanses us of our sinfulness through the application of his precious blood shed for us on Calvary.

The other sacraments are applied at times when we need special grace and strength for a particular purpose. At the beginning of adulthood the Sacrament of Confirmation strengthens the youth in their search for God throughout their lives with the special help and inspiration of the Holy Spirit given to them in fullness. The gifts of the Spirit are given at that crucial moment to enable the youth to handle life from the highest level of their being.

The sacraments of marriage and holy orders enable adults beginning a life of commitment to God and each other in love to sustain their gift amid the vicissitudes of life. It strengthens them against temptations and provides all the help required to live holy and happy lives. Likewise at the term of life we are sent on the final lap of the journey with extreme unction and the Holy Viaticum, the spiritual food for the final lap of the journey. Every moment of our existence has thus been covered with the grace and glory of God. If we do not become holy, it is not His fault, for He has seen to everything. It is up to us to use the means of grace.

DIVINE PROVIDENCE

An essential apsect of growth in holiness is to perceive the presence of God in our daily lives. Otherwise we lose faith, and then hope, and we can walk away from the most important experience of our lives, what we were made for in fact! God watches over His world forever. He who takes care of Israel, His people, neither slumbers nor sleeps, the psalmist says. The theologians tell us that if God removed His hand from creation it would cease to exist. He must continuously keep it in existence, and provide the daily needs for all His creatures. Jesus said that not a hair on our heads can escape His counting! He sees and knows everything.

For the traveller on the road to holiness this means that every step of the way has been taken care of before ever we set out on the way. Jesus IS THE WAY, and has carved out the way to the Father for all of us. We can be absolutely certain that everything we need to obtain the goal of the journey will be provided for us: "Give us today our daily bread . . ." Further, all the grace we need for every situation has been provided by Jesus on Calvary. All we have to do is come to Him in prayer and ask. It is all so simple: Ask and you shall receive, seek and you shall find, knock and the door will be opened unto you . . . (Luke 11.9). This is exactly how children live! They ask for their needs. They talk nicely to their parents about what concerns them, and they expect to get a hearing . . . and the answer to their requests. What parents do for children, Jesus says God does for us all.

The secret is to learn to trust God just as a child trusts his parents. We must trust His goodness, His kindness, His mercy, His faithfulness, etc. Then we have no worries. If only we could say with complete conviction: GOD IS GOOD! all would be well. God's providence would take care of all our needs in the same way as He takes care of the birds in the sky and the fish in the sea. If He can put wool on the back of a sheep, can He not put wool on your back too? Can He not provide for you? Let not our image of God be too small, or we will not be able to believe it when He wants to remove mountains into the sea!

PERSONAL PRAYER

Last, but not least, is the question of personal prayer, on which the relationship with God rests. The spiritual life is a life of personal communication with God. It requires that we spend at least one hour in personal prayer each day if the relationship is to grow and develop. No one else can do this for us, just as no one can breathe our air or eat our food. This is something that we must do for ourselves. Whatever way we pray puts the stamp of individuality on our relationship with God. One must realize from the start that the spiritual life does not survive the absence of prayer.

Prayer can be compared to a coal fire: the more coal is put on it the more light and heat is derived from the fire. But if the fire is neglected it will go out, even if you have the best coal available. Just as a fire needs to be constantly fed with coal, so the spiritual life needs to be constantly fed with prayer. It's about as simple as that.

One needs to set a disciplined timetable to make room for prayer and scripture reading in one's day. It is fatal to hope that you can snatch a few moments at the end of the day when you are tired and unable to concentrate. Prayer should be seen as the priority happening every day, done preferably first thing in the morning, or late at night for those who claim to be "night owls". In either case there needs to be enough silence to be able to hear the Lord.

Go before the Lord just as you are, telling Him who you are and all that concerns you. Talk yourself out in the early days of the relationship, so that you come quickly to that sonorous silence where the Holy Spirit whispers in the depths of your being with sighs and groans too deep for words (Rom. 8.26–27). Do not worry about distractions, just keep bringing your mind back gently, saying to the Lord: "Lord, look at what I was thinking about just now! Bless that situation, that person . . ." and then go on. Base your prayer on the scriptures, either on the gospels or the Psalms, and talk to the Lord about what He is revealing in the text to you. Then take it on from there . . . (I will deal with praying with the scriptures in another booklet.)

There is a saying that we should pray as if everything depended on God, and work as if everything depended on ourselves. This states the delicacy of the sensitivity needed to cooperate with this divine work in our lives.